This book is for parents who desire to become healthier food advocates for themselves and their children.

5-Minute Lunchbox

The busy family's guide to packing deliciously simple, kid-approved healthy lunches.

Kimberly Young, MA
Founder, Healthy Little Cooks

Photography by Naomi Prechtl

Contains 25 fun meals, a weekly shopping list and ingredient substitutions for vegans, vegetarians and many common food allergies.

ISBN-13: 978-0-615-90054-4
ISBN-10: 0-615-90054-2

Published by: Healthy Little Cooks, LLC
P.O. Box 2276
Ellicott City, Maryland 21041
www.HealthyLittleCooks.com

Special Thanks
Food Photography, Naomi Prechtl; InDesign-ers, Tiffany Cole-Stitt and Winston Philip;
Food Editors, J. Scott Wilson, Devona Perrineau and Joyraj D'Souza

Acknowledgments

God, thank you for helping me use my struggle with food to help other kids and their parents learn to respect and appreciate food, family and their body. Ten years ago, I never would have thought about writing a healthy cookbook. But the night you delivered me from my eating disorder, I knew you had an amazing plan for my life. I was destined to help people cook and eat healthier. Thank you Jesus for saving my life in more ways than one and giving me back the ability to enjoy and celebrate food again.

Thanks to my husband Braxton and four beautiful kiddies, Braxton III, Braydon, Bronson and Kaelyn, who support my food experiments (of all kinds). Healthy eating for us has been a journey. You've shown me that it's possible for a mom to change her family's taste buds from unhealthy to healthy. I'm grateful for all of our food aversions, allergies and craziness, because it's those things that have enhanced my culinary skills and inspired me to prepare healthy meals so we can enjoy a better life together. I love all of you.

Mom, you're the perfect example of unconditional love and support. Your heart for helping people and desire to see people happy is energizing and motivating. I'm proud to see you take steps, both big and small, to improve your health despite the difficulties. You're a role model for determination, forgiveness and self-love. You're also an extraordinarily fantastic "grammie!"

Dad, I love you forever! Thanks for teaching me how to make my first real soul food dishes like greens, sweet potatoes and southern pot roast. Your healthy tea concoctions were ahead of their time and are a staple in my diet. I couldn't have prayed for a better dad and friend and am so happy we're able to experience this book together.

My little sister Tiffany, you're an example of how healthy eating can transform someone's life. Thank you for reminding me that there is a difference between healthful eating and healthy eating. You're an inspiration and example of how the right foods can be used for nourishment and healing.

To my BFF Monica, you're the bomb! No other words are necessary (which is why I love you). In a world filled with people who tear each other down, you're a builder. In my life, you've helped build confidence, security, determination and a sense of community. You taught me how essential friends are to living a happy life. As a working mom with three beautiful girls, you were one of my inspirations for writing this book.

Naomi, your ability to bring food to life through pictures is almost the world's best-kept secret and is only outshined by your integrity, sincerity and giving heart. It's been wonderful to see your talent grow into such visual poetry. Thank you for being such a light in my family's life.

Contents

Week One

Avocado, Hummus & Spinach Wrap w/ Applesauce & Pretzels

Chicken & Egg Salad w/ Mixed Fruit & Sesame Sticks

Apple Chicken Sandwich w/ Plantains, Strawberries & Veggies

Fruit Kabobs w/ Raisins, Greek Yogurt & Granola

Leftover Chicken Pizza Pita w/ Dried Mangoes & Broccoli

Week Two

Superhero Sandwich w/ Pretzels, Feta, Apples & Peanut Butter

"BLT" w/ Brown Rice, Black Beans, Yogurt & Fruit

PB&J Sushi w/ Watermelon, Broccoli & Dip

Meatball Sub w/ Popcorn, Spinach Salad & Tangerines

Fruit Pizza w/ Cream Cheese

Week Three

Cucumber Sandwiches w/ Cashews, Grapes & Granola Bar

BBQ Chicken Sandwich w/ Strawberry Salad, Cheese & Pretzels

Guacamole & Chips w/ Apples & Peanut Butter w/ Grapes

Chick'n Sandwich w/ Veggies, Graham Crackers & Oranges

Apples & Peanut Butter w/ Pretzels, Cheese & Veggies w/ Dip

Week Four

Black Bean Burrito w/ Veggies, Oranges & Cottage Cheese

Taco Salad w/ Cheese, Avocado & Salsa

Spiral Festival Pasta w/ Strawberries & Whipped Cream

Egg Salad Sandwich w/ Fruit & Pretzels

Curry Chicken Sandwich w/ Melon & Carrots & Dip

Week Five

Red Bean Dip w/ Flat Pretzels, Pineapple & Veggies

Salmon Salad w/ Cheese, Veggies, Watermelon & Grapes

Dancing Pasta w/ Ants on a Log & a Tangerine

Chicken Sub w/ Chips, Blueberries & Tangerines

Cheese & Crackers w/ Chicken, Broccoli & Fruit

Morning Chaos be Gone

Bringing Healthy Back

Before my kids, I was a morning person. My early waking hours were filled with peace, order and pure enjoyment. But, after having four kids in five years, I found myself dreading those early hours. The "me time" I valued so much became non-existent and was replaced with two hours of breakfast making, lunch packing, diaper changing and dressing my kids. It was pure chaos! I was also on a desperate journey to figure out how to prepare healthy, affordable meals for my family, and it left me scrambling. Desperate for an answer, and not being able to find it anywhere, I decided to create a guide that would help other parents like myself prepare healthier meals for their family that didn't take an hour to prepare. The next day I started writing the 5-Minute Lunchbox.

"I focus on being kind, having fun, enjoying family and living with purpose."

Change is Possible

I love food. But, I think my fascination with food is a little different than most folks in the culinary world. For 13 years, I had an eating disorder, bulimia nervosa, that could have killed me. Then one day when I was at my lowest point in life, on November 4, 2004, I experienced a divine intervention from the Holy Spirit when He delivered me from the illness. Ever since that day, I've committed myself to helping people, specifically women, kids and parents, learn to love themselves and adopt a healthy lifestyle. I used to work hard at being perfect, eating perfectly and doing the perfect things, but that made me tired, impatient and unfulfilled. Now I focus on being kind, having fun, enjoying family and living with purpose.

I love kids. I have four kids, three boys and one girl. I also work with hundreds of kids and parents every year. What I've learned is that most parents want a better life for their kids than what they had themselves. Despite their own unhealthy eating, many parents would love for their kids to be perfect images of health. But the reality is that they are little versions of us. They eat what we eat. Because of that, I believe it's essential that families eat healthy together, which is another reason I created this book. The menus can be modified to meet the dietary needs of toddlers up to active adults. Every meal also comes with suggested food substitutions that address common food allergies and dietary preferences.

I love learning. I'm a self-trained cook and foodie. In my family, we have wheat, nut, tree nut and dairy allergies. I'm 93% vegan (the other 7% vegetarian) and my husband is an omnivore. Since 2005, I've taught and worked with women, parents and kids who have picky taste buds, allergies, special diets, food addictions and/or eating disorders. I'm not a dietitian, but I am Founder and President of Healthy Little Cooks, a mom with a demanding home kitchen, culinary coach, healthy lifestyle blogger, author and wife. I understand the psychological, physical and social impact that food has on our bodies and in our culture. For kids, packing cool foods is an essential component to their lunchtime. For parents, packing healthy foods is essential. This book meets both needs by making lunches fun for kids and healthy and easy for parents.

I love life. I find joy in many things. But, what gets me excited is food, finding a great deal, having fun with my family and seeing people smile. When I'm able to show parents how to cook healthy meals for their families or help kids learn how to cook yummy healthy meals themselves, it makes the world a better place. Food hasn't always been my friend, but it's always been a major player in my life. We can either allow food to give us a better life or make it worse. I want you to have a better life and am confident that this book is packed full of healthy lunch ideas that will help you do just that.

5-Minute Lunchbox Makeover

I've always loved to eat packed lunches from home. Knowing the meal was created specifically for me makes me feel like I'm opening a warm hug from home. Whether it's the fun of opening individual containers, eating my favorite foods or the surprise of seeing what's in my lunchbox, eating a packed lunch has always put a smile on my face.

The 5-Minute Lunchbox helps anyone who wants to pack and eat healthier lunches while at work or school. Each lunchbox week begins with a visual snapshot of all the meals, shopping list and preparation tips. To support on-the-go lifestyles, each meal was developed to fit in a lunchbox and was written with busy parents in mind. The 5-Minute Lunchbox is also an excellent meal-planning guide for day cares, pre-schools, teachers or any adult who wants to pack a healthy lunch.

For many people, packing a healthy lunch is easier to do for themselves than for their family. To complicate matters, if that family has over-busy schedules or members with food allergies, taste aversions or varying eating preferences, mealtime can be even more stressful and complicated.

Whether you are packing for one or eight people, sooner or later the lunch packing experience almost always falls into an unhealthy rut.

This rut, which I call lunch-packing pitfalls, contains 8 categories that if not addressed can lead to a chronically unhealthy lunch.

8 Common Pitfalls of Packing Lunches

1	2	3	4
Boring lunches. You are packing the same thing every day.	**Marathon lunches.** Your healthy lunch takes too long to prepare and pack.	**Semi-healthy lunches.** One healthy item doesn't balance out three unhealthy items.	**Abandoned vegetables.** Your kids are not eating their healthy food options.

5	6	7	8
Problem packer. Your favorite healthy foods don't pack well for on-the-go eating.	**Too expensive.** Your healthy lunches are too expensive to sustain long-term.	**Junk food takeover.** You need help replacing favorite unhealthy treats with healthy foods.	**Foggy brain.** You need help packing healthy foods for kids with allergies or picky eaters.

The 5-Minute Lunchbox changes the lunch-packing experience by removing the pitfalls of packing a lunch and replacing them with 8 beneficial healthy results.

8 Benefits of Using the 5-Minute Lunchbox

1
Fun foods.
Lunches contain variety of easy to find foods.

2
Saves time.
With little weekly prep-work, lunches can be packed in 5 minutes or less.

3
Healthy and balanced.
Most lunches have a B+ or higher overall health rating.

4
Kids eat veggies.
All lunches are kid-approved and fun to eat.

5
Packable foods. Lunches are packable and don't need to be re-heated.

6
Affordable.
Most foods are easy to find and can be bought in bulk.

7
Superhero foods.
Most lunches include a kid-approved healthy treat.

8
Creative alternatives.
There are ingredient substitutions for allergies, vegan and vegetarian preferences.

Lunchbox Guide to Success

5-Minute Lunchbox contains 25 meals broken down over five weeks, which support a Monday-Friday work or school week.

All meals have substitutions that cater to egg, dairy, nut and tree nut allergies.

There are also vegan and vegetarian ingredient substitution suggestions. Although gluten and soy allergies are not directly addressed, because many whole food options are used, the lunchbox meals can be easily customized to fit those dietary needs.

The beginning of each week contains a snapshot picture of the meals, shopping list and prep-work checklist. The typical prep-time averages 25 minutes a week, but can go up to 60 minutes when incorporating some dietary substitutions.

To keep the lunchboxes fun, healthy and exciting, each lunch day has a theme. Daily themes are useful for meal planning. It's also a useful tool for decreasing anxiety in children who may have a difficult time embracing meal or menu changes. If there is a food item or meal that your child dislikes, work together to develop a healthy alternative that they would enjoy and fits the theme.

Meatless Monday: meat-free

Tasty Tuesday: flavorful and colorful

Wacky Wednesday: silly and creative

Terrific Thursday: old-time favorites

Fun Friday: dips, kits and more

Substitutions

All meals are written with ingredient or food substitution suggestions for nut and tree nut allergies, vegan (egg, dairy and meat free) and vegetarian eating. Please use these substitutions as a guide.

Creativity is encouraged. If you're thinking about changing a lunchbox ingredient, go ahead and let your culinary creative juices flow. Just remember to keep a healthier meal focus as your overall objective.

Serving Size

All meals in this book are written to feed one person. The singular serving size makes it easy to increase the amount of ingredients to fit the number of people in your family without requiring you to turn into a mathematician.

Nutritional Info & Health Rating

The nutritional analysis and health ratings were gathered using About.com's calorie count recipe analysis tool. It can be found at *http://caloriecount.about.com/cc/recipe_analysis.php*. Approximately 85% of the ingredients we used in the 5-Minute Lunchbox were found on this website. To include the other 15% of our ingredients used, we compared the manufacturer's label with similar items and selected nutritionally comparable similar items on caloriecount.com. Although caloriecount.com retrieves much of its food's nutritional values from USDA and the food manufacturers, we cannot guarantee the information on caloriecount.com to be 100% accurate. To learn more about how and where caloriecount.com gets its nutritional information, please visit the website: *http://caloriecount.about.com/nutrition-information-foods-q2079*.

Our Ingredients

Because the 5-Minute Lunchbox is a hybrid between a cookbook and meal planner, most of our lunchboxes have ingredients or foods that are sold by different manufacturers and have nutritional variances. When preparing the meals, I selected foods and ingredients that were accessible and had the best nutritional value. When you're shopping, please allow yourself time to read labels and compare the amount of added sugar, sodium, fat and preservatives to pick the healthiest brand available near you.

Disclaimer

I'm not a doctor, physician or dietitian. If you have a medical, mental or health concern, seek the advice of a medical doctor. Do not use this book or information found on www.5MinuteLunchbox.com or www.HealthyLittleCooks.com to replace the advice of your doctor.

Packing safe lunchboxes

Keeping lunches at the right temperature and lunchboxes clean are essential components to packing a healthy lunchbox. Packing food at proper temperatures keeps lunches safe, visually appealing and delicious. Issues that create an unsafe lunchbox are cross-contamination of food with dirty utensils, uncooked food, countertops or storage containers. Be sure to include plenty of ice packs for cold items and insulated containers for hot ones. To help you pack a safe lunchbox, we've included tips with each meal. To learn more about how to pack a safe lunchbox, visit the USDA's website. There is an article called "Keeping Bag Lunches Safe" that provides some great tips at *http://www.fsis.usda.gov/factsheets/Keeping_Bag_Lunches_Safe/index.asp*.

Eco-friendly lunchboxes

Although being kind to our earth is a great gift we can give our future generation, it's also a smart choice that impacts our society and families today. Using reusable containers saves money, creates less trash to haul and makes eating and packing lunchboxes more fun. If you are a newbie at using eco-friendly lunchboxes, start with a thermos, insulated lunch bag, and a couple sets of BPA-free plastic, stainless steel or glass leak-proof containers of various sizes. If you're still on the fence about purchasing reusable containers, I've highlighted some of my favorite benefits of switching to eco-friendly packaging below:

- Keeps food from getting smashed.
- Helps food juices stay where they should be, in the food and not in your lunch bag.
- Creates food ownership mentality, think on-the go plastic forks versus using metal forks.
- Makes packing healthy food easier and more convenient.
- Fun to unpack and eat from.
- Stores leftover foods well (turning them into excellent afternoon snacks!).
- Keeps you healthier. Some plastic bags leak poisonous chemicals into food.
- Helps food taste better. Poisonous chemicals can alter the taste of food.
- Saves you money in the long run.

If you're serious about packing healthier and more affordable lunches, using eco-friendly packaging is a smart choice. However, eco-friendly packaging comes with a few downsides.

Before you start spending money on new lunchbox containers, I've highlighted a few problems that may occur when using them (see following table). Although the concerns are minimal and my solutions are provided below, it wouldn't be fair not to give them a mention.

PROBLEM	SOLUTION
Creates extra dirty dishes	Use a dishwasher or have your kids clean their containers and lunchbox as soon as they get home from school. It will teach responsibility, discipline and involve them in the healthy lunchbox experience.
You wake up and realize that the containers didn't get washed	Purchase an extra set of containers so it doesn't slow you down when you are packing lunches in the morning. Then have your kids wash both sets when they return home from school.
Lids, forks and other utensils magically disappear	Tell your kids that they are responsible for keeping things together and in place. Offer special rewards on Friday if they have kept everything intact and washed all week.
Containers are expensive	Find deals online at *www.HealthyLittleCooks.com*, it's worth the investment. Containers give you more food-packing flexibility. In the long run, you'll end up spending less money than using pre-packaged food items or plastic bags.
Containers take up cabinet space	Store them in your lunch bag.

Frequently Asked Questions

Q: Have you made these recipes before? Are you sure they only take 5 minutes?

A: Yes, I've made 100% of them and as long as you do the suggested prep work (15-60 minutes a week), the lunches only take 5 minutes to prepare.

Q: What about kids with allergies? Will this book help them?

A: All recipes have ingredient substitutions for vegan and vegetarian lifestyles along with nut/tree nut, dairy, egg and milk allergies. One of my sons has a severe nut/tree nut allergy and wheat intolerance, so I'm extra sensitive to kids who have allergies and supporting the parents who love them.

Q: Does this book give options for kids with gluten or wheat allergies?

A: I'm working on a special project for families with gluten and wheat allergies. Until then, because we use so many whole foods in the 5-Minute Lunchbox, many meals can be easily modified to fit a GF lifestyle.

Q: What about picky kids? Will they like these meals?

A: Each lunchbox has a tip for parents of picky eaters. Also, if you see an ingredient that your child does not like, substitute it for a healthy replacement they'll eat.

Q: Certain foods are repeated; what about exposing kids to different foods?

A: There are certain foods, such as pretzels, repeated throughout the book. Although they are not a nutrient dense food, I use pretzels for a few reasons: 1) most kids love pretzels; 2) the low fat content makes them healthier than potato chips; 3) they are extremely affordable; and 4) they have a long shelf life. The goal in the 5-Minute Lunchbox is to help you prepare nutritious, fun meals that kids will love. To do that, there sometimes has to be a healthy compromise. However, after assessing your family's nutritional needs, please feel free to swap any item for something that better supports your dietary needs.

Q: Am I getting enough protein in some of these meals?

A: Although many meals do not contain meat, they do have protein. Remember that protein comes in a variety of different foods such as beans, high-protein bread and pasta. If you still feel after reading the nutritional information that you need more protein, feel free to add your favorite type of protein to the meal. The 5-Minute Lunchbox meals can be modified to fit your taste buds and appetite.

Q: Why do you only offer five meals each week?

A: Most packed lunches are eaten at school or work. The 5-Minute Lunchbox was written to offer healthy meal solutions to overcome the lunchtime rut when packing lunches.

Q: Why did we keep brand names of the foods we used a secret?

1. Nutritional needs, allergies and dietary preferences such as vegan or vegetarian lifestyles vary from person to person. There's no one super brand or food (besides water) that caters to the medical and dietary needs of everyone.
2. Availability of certain foods or brand names may vary. This book was written to make packing lunches easier, not to be a task that requires you to transform into a grocery store detective, scouring the aisles looking for the perfect ingredient.
3. Factors such as new products, research and medical needs determine which brands are healthiest for an individual. For example, a food allergy can turn traditionally healthy foods into a life-threatening situation.

Set the Healthy Eating Tone

What's healthy?

I do my best to promote and create healthy meals. But I also understand that healthy doesn't mean the same thing to all people. This is especially true when food allergies or other medical issues are a factor. The varying dietary needs, health issues, diets and eating preferences can make "healthy" a battleground word, which is why I prefer the term "healthier." Healthier meets a person where he or she is and empowers them with the knowledge and confidence to make changes that lead to their optimal health. If you want to live a healthier lifestyle, it's essential that you find the eating plan that works for your body.

After many years of exploring food, a vegan diet works best for me. However, my choice may not be the best for everyone—a vegan diet requires careful consideration and can have nutrition pitfalls, such as eating an insufficient amount of protein, too much sugar or high-fat foods. The fact is that unhealthy options exist in almost every eating lifestyle. To become a healthier you and find balance, focus on four areas.

1. Focus on the types of foods you are eating.
2. Pay attention to how those foods make you feel and your attitudes surrounding them.
3. Opt out of defining yourself with a food label.
4. Focus on eating foods that make you feel good.

> **Whether you're searching for optimal health or simply creating healthier meals, I truly believe this book will help you and your family enter into a healthier lifestyle.**

Avocado, Hummus and Spinach Wrap with Applesauce and Pretzels

Chicken and Egg Salad with Mixed Fruit and Sesame Sticks

Chicken Apple Sandwich with Plantains, Strawberries and Veggies

Fruit Kabobs with Raisins, Greek Yogurt and Granola

Chicken Pizza Pita with Dried Mangoes and Broccoli

Shopping List

week1

1

Grocery

Hummus
100-calorie whole-wheat tortillas
Mayonnaise (regular or vegan)
Mustard
Pretzel sticks
Applesauce (unsweetened)
Granola (nut-free if allergies are a concern) *
Sunflower butter (optional)
1 tablespoon sesame seeds
2 baked mini breadsticks
Raisins
Marinara sauce
100-calorie whole-wheat bagel
Whole-wheat pita pocket
Plantain chips (optional)
Low-fat granola bar *
Kabob sticks (or wooden skewers)

Produce

1 avocado
1 cup spinach
Raw almonds (optional)
Precut romaine lettuce with mixed vegetables
Cherry tomatoes
1 cucumber

Watermelon
Cantaloupe
Honeydew melon
Grapes
Pineapple
Strawberries
1 apple
1 stalk celery
Carrots
Dried mango slices

Dairy

Eggs **
1/4 cup 2% shredded mozzarella cheese (or non-dairy cheese)
Fat-free Greek vanilla yogurt

Meat

1 chicken breast or
6 ounces frozen precooked breast strips (may substitute vegan or vegetarian "chicken")

*Item is optional and can be replaced for DIY Granola, an optional substitution for anyone who wishes to make his or her own granola. The ingredients are not on this shopping list, but can be seen on page 74.

**Item is optional and can be replaced with Eggless Dill Salad, an optional meal substitution for vegan and vegetarian diets. The ingredients for this recipe are not on this list, but can be seen on page 72.

Prep Work

Week1

1

 *10 minutes – 1 hour*

Review this week's menu.

Then use the following prep-work chart as a guide.
Modify it to fit your specific taste buds, fruit in season or on sale and recommended lunchbox allergy or food substitution as desired.

Task	Time	This Is For
Wash fruits and vegetables	2 minutes	Everyone
Dice 1/4 cup celery and 1/4 cup carrots	3 minutes	Everyone
Hard boil 1 egg	12 minutes	Everyone, except vegetarians
Dice fruit into 1-inch cubes (watermelon, melon, pineapple)	5 minutes	Everyone
Bake chicken breast (cut 1/4 cup into strips and 1/3 cup into chunks)	25 minutes *	Everyone, except vegans and vegetarians
Prepare Eggless Dill Salad (optional substitution)	20 minutes *	Vegans and vegetarians substitutions
Make DIY granola	25 minutes *	Everyone (optional)

*To save time, these items can be done in conjunction with other prep work such as chopping, dicing, or pre-mixing ingredients.

Avocado, Hummus and Spinach Wrap with Applesauce and Pretzels

Grab

Avocado, Hummus and Spinach Wrap

1/4 avocado
1 cup spinach
2 tablespoons hummus
1/4 cup chopped tomato
1 100% whole-wheat 100-calorie tortilla
1 teaspoon mayonnaise (optional)
Mustard

Sides

1 oz pretzel sticks (about 53 pretzels)
1/2 cup unsweetened applesauce

Food Allergy Tips & Substitutions

For vegan and vegetarian diets and most allergies, adopt the substitution that fits your needs.

Replace regular mayonnaise with a vegan brand. If you're new at shopping for allergy-free foods, be sure to check ingredient labels. Some tortillas contain or are made in a factory with nuts, tree nuts, milk or soy products.

How to Make It

Spread hummus on tortilla. Layer with spinach, chopped avocado, tomatoes and mustard. Roll tightly and pack in an individual container.

Picky Eater Tip

Because of its smooth yet firm texture, avocados may take your little eater some time to get used to. If this describes your kid, dice the avocado in small pieces, or mash it and spread it on your tortilla like mayonnaise. Their taste buds will get used to the flavor without the fuss.

Feed the Sweet Tooth

Applesauce is an excellent natural way to feed a sweet tooth. Just purchase the no-sugar-added variety. Also, when making your own, top it with a dash of cinnamon or nutmeg, diced fruit or nuts to add extra flavor and crunch.

Larger Appetites

Add 10 raw almonds and gain 69 calories and 2.5 grams of protein. If nuts are an issue, add one tablespoon of sunflower butter as a pretzel dip for an afternoon snack. But be aware you'll be adding 100 calories and 3.5 grams of protein.

Nutrition Information

Calories 420, Total Fat 13.5g, Sat Fat 1.8g, Trans Fat 0g, Cholesterol 1mg, Sodium 980mg, Carbohydrates 73g, Fiber 16.8g, Sugar 18.2g, Protein 12.9g, Vitamin A 65%, Calcium 27%, Vitamin C 33%, Iron 31%: Nutritional Grade B+

Nutrition Tip

For the person that isn't a huge hummus fan, mayonnaise gives this sandwich a familiar creamy taste. If this describes your household, work toward eliminating the mayonnaise to save 25 calories and 2 grams of fat.

Tasty Tuesday

Chicken and Egg Salad with Mixed Fruit and Sesame Sticks

Grab

Chicken-Egg Salad

1 hardboiled egg
2 cups precut romaine lettuce with shredded vegetables
4 cherry tomatoes
1/4 cup baked chicken breast strips
*2 tablespoons of low-fat or fat-free dressing of your choice

Mixed Fruit

1/4 cup watermelon, diced
1/4 cup grapes, diced
1/4 cup honeydew melon, diced
1/4 cup pineapple, diced

Sides

2 tablespoons 2% shredded mozzarella cheese (optional)
1 tablespoon toasted sesame seeds
2 baked mini breadsticks – optional for larger appetites

Food Allergy Tips & Substitutions

For vegan and vegetarian diets and most allergies, adopt the substitution that fits your needs.

Swap baked chicken strips with 4 vegan or vegetarian chicken strips. Omit egg. Replace 2% shredded mozzarella cheese with your favorite non-dairy or vegan brand.

How to Make Chicken-Egg Salad

Place lettuce in a bowl, and then top it with tomatoes, chicken and hardboiled egg. Pack dressing on the side.

How to Make Mixed Fruit

Combine all ingredients to make one delicious cup of fruit.

Packing Tip

Create your own do-it-yourself lunchbox by packing the chicken, low-fat dressing, cheese and sesame seeds in their own container. The more kids are involved in making their meal, the more they'll eat it.

Picky Eater Tip

Do your best to try and keep sesame seeds in this meal. They are an excellent source of protein, fiber and contain as much calcium as a half-cup of milk.

Total Lunchbox Nutrition Information

Calories 447, Total Fat 18.7, Sat Fat 4.9g, Trans Fat 0g, Cholesterol 207mg, Sodium 465mg, Carbohydrates 53.6, Fiber 11.2g, Sugar 29.3g, Protein 33.5g, Vitamin A 233%, Calcium 25%, Vitamin C 186%, Iron 36%: Nutritional Grade A

*Dressing is not included.

Nutrition Tip

This hearty and well-balanced meal is packed full of fruits, vegetables and lean protein and is rated nutritional grade A. But, if you're watching your calorie intake, eliminate the breadsticks to save 80 calories and 4 grams of fat.

1 Wacky Wednesday

Chicken Apple Sandwich with Plantains, Strawberries and Veggies

Grab

Chicken Apple Sandwich

1/3 cup diced chicken breast
1 tablespoon diced apples
1/2 tablespoon raisins
1/2 tablespoon chopped celery
1 tablespoon mayonnaise
100 calorie whole-wheat bagel

Sides

1/3 cup plantain chips – optional for
    larger appetites
1 low-fat granola bar
3 cherry tomatoes
4 slices cucumbers

Food Allergy Tips & Substitutions

For vegan and vegetarian diets
and most allergies, adopt the
substitution that fits your needs.

To go meatless, replace chicken
with grilled tofu. Or, prepare our
Eggless Dill Salad (pg 72) over the
weekend.

How to Make It
Combine diced chicken breast with apples, raisins,
celery, mayonnaise and a dash of pepper in a bowl
and mix well. Then spread it on your bagel.

Packing Tip
Make it visually fun! Pack everything individually so
your little one can eat with his or her eyes first!

Picky Eater Tip
For kids that dislike tomatoes, swap them out for red
peppers, which also have lycopene.

Feed the Sweet Tooth
If you eliminate the plantains, but want an extra boost
of sweetness, add a tablespoon of whipped cream
as dip for the strawberries.

Total Lunchbox Nutrition Information
Calories 494, Total Fat 14.8, Sat Fat 2.2g, Trans Fat 0g,
Cholesterol 68mg, Sodium 684mg, Carbohydrates
66g, Fiber 9g, Sugar 12.4g, Protein 23g, Vitamin A 2%,
Calcium 15%, Vitamin C 50%, Iron 18%: Nutritional
Grade B+

Nutrition Tip

Some varieties of plantain chips can contain up to 100 calories and 5 grams of fat. Only recommend for active teens or adults, but if you can't go without this extra finger-food, decrease the serving to 1/4 cup or swap it for low-fat popcorn.

1 Terrific Thursday

Fruit Kabobs with Raisins, Greek Yogurt and Granola

Grab

Fruit Kabob

1/4 cup grapes
1/4 cup melons, cantaloupe
1/4 cup watermelon
1/4 cup pineapple
1/4 cup strawberries
2 wooden kabob sticks

Sides

1/3 cup low-fat granola cereal
1/8 cup raisins
1/2 cup fat-free vanilla Greek
  yogurt

Food Allergy Tips & Substitutions

For vegan and vegetarian diets and most allergies, adopt the substitution that fits your needs.

Replace Greek yogurt with soy or almond yogurt. Supplement the protein you're losing from swapping out the Greek yogurt by using high-protein granola. For nut allergies, purchase nut-free granola or make our DIY granola (pg 74).

How to Make It

Cut off ends of wooden kabob stick to fit in lunchbox. Thread with fruit, alternating the pieces until you run out of room on the stick.

Packing Tip

Pack kabobs in an airtight container or wrap them in plastic wrap and again in foil. Pack the rest of your ingredients separately.

Picky Eater Tip

This lunchbox gets no complaints from most kids. But, if you have a protester, swap out fruits they dislike for their favorites. Try to make the kabob as vibrant as possible, because each color provides a different nutritional benefit.

Feed the Sweet Tooth

The fruit in this meal will feed your sweet tooth, so when adding granola, chose a cereal that has 5 grams of sugar or less. If you are having trouble finding 100% granola, look for high-fiber cereals with whole grains as a substitute.

Larger Appetites

Add a few extra pieces of fruit, nuts, soy nuts or sesame seeds.

Total Lunchbox Nutrition Information

Calories 444, Total Fat 10.2, Sat Fat 1.7g, Trans Fat 0g, Cholesterol 0mg, Sodium 95mg, Carbohydrates 66g, Fiber 6.3g, Sugar 29.3g, Protein 23.8g, Vitamin A 32%, Calcium 26%, Vitamin C 98%, Iron 14%: Nutritional Grade A

Nutrition Tip

Making your own granola is a healthy way to get the nutritional benefits from oats without the added sugar typically hidden in store-bought granola. Be sure to purchase a high-protein variety or try my DIY Granola recipe on page 74.

Leftover Chicken Pizza Pita with Dried Mangoes and Broccoli

Grab

Chicken Pizza Pita

1/2 whole wheat pita pocket
1/2 cup diced chicken
1/4 cup diced carrots
2 Tablespoons low-fat mozzarella cheese
2 Tablespoons marinara sauce

Sides

6 dried mango slices
1 tablespoon raisins or cranberries
1/3 cup chopped broccoli
100 calorie low-fat granola bar
   (optional for larger appetites)

Food Allergy Tips & Substitutions

For vegan and vegetarian diets and most allergies, adopt the substitution that fits your needs.

Replace diced chicken with vegetarian or vegan chicken cutlets. Either omit the mozzarella cheese or replace it with your favorite vegan or non-dairy variety.

How to Make It
To increase this lunchbox's fun factor, let your kids put it together themselves.

Packing Tip
Pack everything in separate containers. If you're running out of containers or bags, combine the chicken and carrots.

Feed the Sweet Tooth
Dried fruits and vegetables are extremely convenient and are naturally sweetened. But, they can be costly. Substitute fresh grapes or any fruit in season or on sale for the dried mangoes in this lunchbox. The natural juices will make your sweet tooth and digestive system equally happy.

Larger Appetites
This is a pretty hearty meal. Portion control is important in healthy eating, so unless you need to pack something extra for snack time, try not to add anything else to this lunchbox.

Total Lunchbox Nutrition Information
Calories 528, Total Fat 10, Sat Fat 3.8g, Trans Fat 0g, Cholesterol 70mg, Sodium 515mg, Carbohydrates 86g, Fiber 10.2g, Sugar 35g, Protein 34g, Vitamin A 132%, Calcium 27%, Vitamin C 145%, Iron 14%: Nutritional Grade B+

Nutrition Tip

Taste the sweetness without the added sugar by purchasing unsweetened dried fruit or dried fruit sweetened with juice instead of sugar.

Meatless Monday

Superhero Sandwich with Pretzels, Feta, Apples and Peanut Butter

Tasty Tuesday

BLT with Brown Rice, Black Beans, Yogurt and Fruit

Wacky Wednesday

PB&J Sushi with watermelon, broccoli and dip

Terrific Thursday

Meatball Sub with Popcorn, Spinach Salad and Tangerine

Fun Friday

Fruit Pizza with Cream Cheese

Grocery

100-calorie whole-wheat bagels
Whole-wheat bread
Whole-wheat hot dog buns
Whole-wheat raisin English muffin
Jelly of your choice
Brown rice
Black beans
Mustard
Mayonnaise (or vegan mayonnaise)
Marinara sauce
Mini pretzel twists
Low-fat popcorn
Peanut butter (substitute soy butter or sunflower butter if allergies are an issue)
Low-fat ranch dressing (or vegan dressing)

Produce

Cucumber
Tomatoes
Cherry tomatoes
Shredded carrots
Red onion
Romaine lettuce
Apple
Grapes
Strawberries
Blueberries
Leaf spinach
Tangerines
Pineapple
Almonds (optional)
Sunflower seeds (optional)
Watermelon
Broccoli
Shaved almonds (or sunflower seeds, flax seeds or crushed soy nuts)

Dairy

Low-fat feta cheese (substitute shaved almonds for vegan or allergy concerns)
Yogurt
String cheese (optional)
Low-fat mozzarella cheese
Low-fat cream cheese (or non-dairy cream cheese)

Meat

Veggie bacon
Pre-cooked turkey meatballs (or meatless ones)

Prep Work

week 2

2

 9 minutes — 20 minutes

Review this week's menu.

Then use the following prep-work chart as a guide.
Modify it to fit your specific taste buds, fruit in season (or on sale)
and recommended lunchbox allergy or food substitution as
desired.

Task	Time	This Is For
Wash fruits and vegetables	2 minutes	Everyone
Slice cucumbers (6 slices)	1 minutes	Everyone
Pre-cook brown rice	20 minutes *	Everyone, unless you have frozen, or prepared rice
Dice watermelon and pineapple into small pieces	5 minutes	Everyone
Dice broccoli florets	3 minutes	Everyone, unless you purchased the pre-cut version

*To save time, these items can be done in conjunction with other
prep work such as chopping, dicing, or pre-mixing ingredients.

This Food Loves You

2 Meatless Monday

Superhero Sandwich with Pretzels, Feta, Apples and Peanut Butter

Grab

Superhero Sandwich

1 100-calorie whole-wheat bagel
6 cucumber slices
6 carrot slices
2 tomato slices
2 slices of red onion
1 leaf romaine lettuce
1 tablespoon low-fat feta cheese
1 teaspoon mustard
1 teaspoon mayonnaise

Sides

1 apple
20 mini pretzel twists (one serving)
1 tablespoon peanut butter

Food Allergy Tips & Substitutions

For vegan and vegetarian diets and most allergies, adopt the substitution that fits your needs.

Swap the feta cheese for shaved almonds (for added calcium). Use vegan mayonnaise. Replace peanut butter with Sunflower butter or soy nut butter.

How to Make It

Spread mayonnaise and mustard on both sides of bread. Add cucumbers, carrots, tomatoes and onions.

Packing Tip

To make this lunchbox fun for kids, pack the feta cheese on the side and let them sprinkle it on their sandwich. The more kids are involved in preparing their meals, the more they will enjoy eating it! Pack everything else separately as shown.

Picky Eater Tip

Onions can be hard to swallow for some kids. If this describes your little eaters, leave them out. Apply the same rule if there is another veggie on this sandwich that displeases their taste buds. To avoid a battle, simply ask them which veggie they would like to eat in place of the one they don't like. They'll be happy that you included them in their lunch-packing process and you'll be happy they are eating veggies for lunch.

Larger Appetites

This should satisfy most appetites, but if more is needed, add a few extra cucumbers on the side. The crunch will satisfy the desire to chew and add only 10 calories.

Total Lunchbox Nutrition Information

Calories 478, Total Fat 13.3, Sat Fat 2.6, Trans Fat 0g, Cholesterol 5mg, Sodium 838mg, Carbohydrates 80g, Fiber 12g, Sugar 22g, Protein 14.7g, Vitamin A 7%, Calcium 11%, Vitamin C 21%, Iron 18%: Nutritional Grade B

Nutrition Tip

Most kids love anything that reminds them of a superhero, but if you have a little princess, tell her she's eating a Princess Sandwich. Pick the vegetables she enjoys most and wrap it with a pink ribbon. She'll be sure to eat her royal sandwich this day!

2 Tasty Tuesday

Veggie BLT with Brown Rice, Black Beans, Yogurt and Fruit

Grab

Veggie BLT

1 leaf of romaine lettuce
2 slices of tomatoes
3 slices of veggie bacon
1 teaspoon of mayonnaise
2 slices of 100-calorie sandwich
   bread

Rice & Beans

1/2 cup brown rice
1/3 cup black beans
1/3 cup spinach (chopped)
1 tablespoon low-fat feta cheese
Optional: fresh parsley, cilantro or
   basil, cumin or onion powder

Sides

1 tangerine
1/4 cup fresh pineapple
1/2 cup or tube yogurt

Food Allergy Tips & Substitutions

For vegan and vegetarian diets
and most allergies, adopt the
substitution that fits your needs.

Use vegan mayonnaise. Eliminate
feta cheese or swap it for an
equal portion of sesame seeds.

How to Make Veggie "BLT"

Spread mayonnaise on one slice of bread. On that
same piece, lay veggie turkey bacon, onions and
tomatoes. On the other slice add lettuce. Be sure to
keep lettuce on the dry side of your sandwich so it
doesn't wilt. Close your sandwich and pack it.

How to Make Rice and Beans

Mix brown rice with beans and spinach. For an extra
boost of flavor, add herbs, onion powder or cumin
(and salt to taste). Top with feta cheese.

Packing Tip

Pack all ingredients in a separate container. Store
fruit in an airtight container to prevent it from leaking.
Include ice packs to keep your food safe and fresh.

Feed the Sweet Tooth

Opt-out of the flavored yogurt insanity and buy
the plain or no-sugar variety. Add a tablespoon of
frozen 100% orange or apple juice on top as healthy
sweetener.

Larger Appetites

Depending on dietary needs, add a piece of string
cheese, 10 almonds or two tablespoons of sunflower
seeds mixed with raisins.

Total Lunchbox Nutrition Information

Calories 475, Total Fat 7.8, Sat Fat 0.8g, Trans Fat 0g,
Cholesterol 6mg, Sodium 871mg, Carbohydrates
87g, Fiber 13g, Sugar 29g, Protein 21g, Vitamin A 22%,
Calcium 24%, Vitamin C 91%, Iron 16%: Nutritional
Grade B+

Nutrition Tip

All yogurts are not created equally. Some have added food coloring, high amounts of sugar or filler ingredients. When searching for the healthiest yogurt available be sure check the sugar and protein amounts.

2 Wacky Wednesday

PB&J Sushi with Watermelon, Broccoli and Dip

Grab

PB&J Sushi

2 slices of 100% whole wheat bread
1 tablespoon of your favorite jelly (low-sugar)
1 tablespoon of peanut butter

Sides

1 cup diced watermelon
1/3 cup of fresh broccoli florets
1 tablespoon of low-fat ranch dressing

Food Allergy Tips & Substitutions

For vegan and vegetarian diets and most allergies, adopt the substitution that fits your needs.

Replace low-fat ranch dressing with vegan dressing. Swap peanut butter for sunflower butter or soy nut butter.

How to Make It

Separately flatten each piece of bread with a rolling pin, can or your hand. Add peanut butter on one piece of bread and jelly on the other. Close the pieces of bread on top of each other and roll very tightly. Then slice into 1/4 inch pieces.

Packing Tip

Pack everything in a separate container. Be sure to use plenty of ice to keep your ranch dip safe and fruits and vegetables fresh.

Feed the Sweet Tooth

The diced watermelon and jelly on the sushi roll should fix the sweet tooth. Try not to pack any additional sugar in this lunch.

Larger Appetites

Add a piece of string cheese to the meal. For a non-dairy option, add a mix of 10 almonds and raisins. For a nut-free option, add mix of two tablespoons of sunflower seeds and raisins.

Total Lunchbox Nutrition Information

Calories 387, Total Fat 13, Sat Fat 2.6g, Trans Fat 0g, Cholesterol 0mg, Sodium 485mg, Carbohydrates 56g, Fiber 6.3g, Sugar 35.3g, Protein 18g, Vitamin A 20%, Calcium 8%, Vitamin C 69%, Iron 14%: Nutritional Grade B+

Nutrition Tip

Make this sandwich a little healthier by swapping jelly for a thinly sliced banana or finely diced apples. This gives a bite of natural sweetness without the added sugar.

2 Terrific Thursday

Meatball Sub with Popcorn, Spinach Salad and Tangerine

Grab

Meatball Sub

3 turkey or meatless meatballs
1 whole-wheat hot dog bun
1/4 cup marinara sauce.

Spinach Salad

1 cup spinach
6 cherry tomatoes
1/4 cup shredded carrots
* Favorite low-fat dressing

Food Allergy Tips & Substitutions

For vegan and vegetarian diets and most allergies, adopt the substitution that fits your needs.

Read your ingredients on the popcorn. Some are made with butter (a milk product). Swap out turkey meatballs for a vegetarian or vegan brand.

How to Make the Meatball Sub

Warm both meatballs and marinara sauce separately in the microwave until hot. Once finished cooking, immediately place meatballs on the bun and wrap in foil or insulated container. Keep the bread from becoming soggy by packing the warmed marinara sauce separately in an insulated container. Do not warm the bun.

How to Make Spinach Salad

Place spinach in a bowl and top it with tomatoes and shredded carrots. Pack your dressing in a small leak-proof container on the side.

Packing Tip

If you only have one insulated container, save yourself a step and pack the marinara sauce and meatballs together and wrap the bun separately. Remember to show your kids a picture of this lunchbox so they will know how it should be assembled.

Picky Eater Tip

If you're still trying to convince your kids to eat salads, start slowly by replacing it with their favorite two or three uncooked vegetables such as carrots, chopped cauliflower, snap peas or tomatoes.

Total Lunchbox Nutrition Information

Calories 423, Total Fat 12, Sat Fat 3.1g, Trans Fat 0g, Cholesterol 2mg, Sodium 1014mg, Carbohydrates 61g, Fiber 17.3g, Sugar 23g, Protein 29g, Vitamin A 177%, Calcium 40%, Vitamin C 96%, Iron 57%: Nutritional Grade A-

* Dressing is not included.

Fun Friday

Fruit Pizza with Cream Cheese

Grab

Fruit Pizza

1/3 cup grapes
1/3 cup strawberries, diced
1/3 cup diced pineapple
1/3 cup blueberries
1 tablespoon shaved almonds
1 tablespoon low-fat cream cheese
1 100% whole wheat raisin English muffin

Food Allergy Tips & Substitutions

For vegan and vegetarian diets and most allergies, adopt the substitution that fits your needs.

Replace regular cream cheese with non-dairy cream cheese. Replace almonds with sunflower seeds, flax seeds or crushed soy nuts.

How to Make It

This is my favorite DIY lunch. Pack all the fruit in one leak-proof container. Slice the English muffin and place it in a separate container. Pack both the shaved almonds and cream cheese in separate containers.

Packing Tip

Remember to include a knife to spread the cream cheese, and for younger kids, explain to them how to assemble the fruit pizza in the morning before school.

Picky Eater Tip

Turn this into a no-fuss recipe by using your kid's favorite fruits. If raisin muffins are the source of their anxiety, swap them for a 100% whole-wheat or whole-grain version.

Larger Appetites

Mix in an extra tablespoon of almonds, raisins or sunflower seeds. Or include a small spinach and tomato salad on the side.

Total Lunchbox Nutrition Information

Calories 345, Total Fat 6.6, Sat Fat 1.7g, Trans Fat 0g, Cholesterol 7mg, Sodium 242mg, Carbohydrates 62g, Fiber 8g, Sugar 29.3g, Protein 11g, Vitamin A 6%, Calcium 11%, Vitamin C 98%, Iron 15%: Nutritional Grade B

Nutrition Tip

This fun lunchbox contains a lot of natural sugar, so to cut back without losing flavor, purchase muffins with no or low added sugar and use two fruits versus four. Also, double the amount of almonds or add one tablespoon of walnuts for extra protein.

Shopping List

week 3

3

Meatless Monday

Cucumber Sandwiches with Cashews, Grapes and Granola Bar

Tasty Tuesday

BBQ Chicken Sandwich with Cheese, Strawberry Salad and Pretzels

Wacky Wednesday

Guacamole and Chips with Apples and Peanut Butter with Grapes

Terrific Thursday

Chick'n Sandwich with Veggies, Graham Crackers and Oranges

Fun Friday

Apples & Peanut Butter with Pretzels, Cheese and Veggies with Dip

Grocery

Whole-wheat bread
Whole-wheat bagel
Whole-wheat hamburger bun
Rice crispy treat*
Mini graham crackers
Cashews (or sunflower seeds pumpkin seeds or crushed soy nuts)
Barbecue sauce
Low-fat Italian dressing
Low-fat ranch dressing
Pretzel sticks
Mini pretzel twists
Tortilla chips
Peanut butter (use soy nut or sunflower butter if allergies are an issue)
Lemon juice
Ketchup
Mustard
Cinnamon

Produce

Cucumber
Avocado
Tomato
Lettuce
Yellow onion
Cherry tomatoes
Shredded red cabbage
Baby spinach
Carrot sticks or Mini Carrots
Celery sticks
Snap peas
Dried dill or chives
Cilantro
Lime
Grapes
Apple
Orange
Strawberries
Blueberries

Dairy

Whipped cream cheese (or non-dairy cream cheese or low-fat mayonnaise)
Low-fat shredded mozzarella cheese (for dairy allergy substitution swap for sesame seeds)
2% milk American cheese slices, Low-fat marble cheese or Cheddar cheese, cubed (money-saver tip: substitute for 2 slices of American cheese slices)
1% milk (or milk substitute)

Meat

1 chicken breast (grilled tofu or shredded seitan for vegan menus)
Veggie burger

*Item is optional and can be replaced for your own favorite rice crispy treat recipe or our DIY Granola, an optional substitution for anyone who wishes to make his or her own granola. The ingredients are not on this shopping list, but can be seen on page 74.

Prep Work

Week 3

3

 3 minutes – 25 minutes

Review this week's menu.

Then use the following prep-work chart as a guide.
Modify it to fit your specific taste buds, fruit in season or on sale and recommended lunchbox allergy or food substitution as desired.

Task	Time	This Is For
Wash fruits and vegetables	2 minutes	Everyone
Slice cucumbers (4 slices)	1 minutes	Everyone
Bake a chicken breast (cut 1/4 cup into strips and 1/3 cup into chunks)	25 minutes *	Everyone, except vegans and vegetarians

*To save time, these items can be done in conjunction with other prep work such as chopping, dicing, or pre-mixing ingredients.

3 Meatless Monday

Cucumber Sandwiches with Cashews, Grapes and Granola Bar

Grab

Cucumber Sandwich

2 slices of whole-wheat bread
4 thick slices of cucumbers
4 cherry tomatoes, sliced in half
1/4 cup red shredded cabbage
1 tablespoon whipped cream cheese
1 teaspoon dried dill or chives

Sides

1 Rice crispy treat
1/8 cup cashews
1/2 cup grapes

Food Allergy Tips & Substitutions

For vegan and vegetarian diets and most allergies, adopt the substitution that fits your needs.

Replace regular cream cheese with non-dairy cream cheese or low-fat mayonnaise. Replace cashews with sunflower seeds, pumpkin seeds or crushed soy nuts.

How to Make It

Cut the crusts off your bread then cut it in quarters (you should have 8 mini pieces of bread). Spread a small amount of cream cheese on all 8 pieces of bread and sprinkle with dill. Place one sliced cucumber, one sliced cherry tomato (2 halves) and a quarter of your cabbage on one piece of bread and top with another piece of bread. Repeat the process to make 4 mini sandwiches total.

Packing Tip

If your sandwiches are falling apart, stick a toothpick in the middle of each mini sandwich to keep them together. Pack separately in a container.

Picky Eater Tip

Encourage your child to eat these fun sandwiches by making faces on top using small cut-up pieces of carrots and cucumbers.

Larger Appetites

If you're feeling "meaty" cook two pieces of veggie bacon (to keep it meatless) and divide it into fours and add it to your mini sandwiches.

Total Lunchbox Nutrition Information

Calories 394, Total Fat 15, Sat Fat 5g, Trans Fat 0g, Cholesterol 11mg, Sodium 174mg, Carbohydrates 60g, Fiber 10g, Sugar 29g, Protein 10g, Vitamin A 107%, Calcium 190%, Vitamin C 12%, Iron 19%: Nutritional Grade A-

Nutrition Tip

If you're in a pinch and need to swap out red cabbage, replace it with (or add) baby spinach. You'll be getting similar nutritional benefits, slightly less vitamin C, but more protein, iron, folate, manganese and vitamin K.

3 Tasty Tuesday

BBQ Chicken Sandwich with Cheese, Strawberry Salad and Pretzels

Grab

BBQ Chicken

1 100% whole-wheat bagel
1/2 cup cooked chicken breast, chopped
1 tablespoon barbecue sauce

Spinach Salad

1 cup baby spinach
1/2 cup strawberries, halved
1/4 cup blueberries
1 tablespoon low-fat Italian dressing of your choice

Sides

18 stick pretzels (one serving)
5 cubes low-fat marble cheese (one serving)

Food Allergy Tips & Substitutions

For vegan and vegetarian diets and most allergies, adopt the substitution that fits your needs.

Swap chicken breast for grilled tofu or shredded seitan. Eliminate mozzarella cheese or replace it with sesame seeds.

How to Make Spinach Salad

Warm chopped chicken breast in the microwave. Then, mix it with barbecue sauce and pack in a small insulated container. Keep bagel fresh by packing it in an airtight container.

Packing Tip

Satisfy little ones' taste buds by allowing them to assemble this lunchbox meal themselves. Pack the Spinach Salad, cheese and pretzels separately.

Picky Eater Tip

If your kids have a hard time eating salad, turn lunchtime eating into a game. Each time they eat all of their salad at lunch, give them a star. At the end of the week, if they've earned 5 stars, then take them on a special trip to the park, swimming pool, zoo or other favorite activity. If that doesn't excite them, then find something that will such as earning a dollar or a pack of stickers for 5 stars.

Feed the Sweet Tooth

The strawberries and blueberries should feed your sweet tooth. But, if you need a little more, add a piece of sugar-free gum.

Total Lunchbox Nutrition Information

Calories 410, Total Fat 8, Sat Fat 1.7g, Trans Fat 0g, Cholesterol 72mg, Sodium 856mg, Carbohydrates 52g, Fiber 6.4g, Sugar 13g, Protein 35g, Vitamin A 62%, Calcium 22%, Vitamin C 91%, Iron 26%: Nutritional Grade A

Nutrition Tip

Be sure to read the label on your bagel package. Unless it says 100% whole-wheat, it could contain mostly processed or white flour, which has less nutritional benefits.

3 Wacky Wednesday

Guacamole and Chips with Apples, Peanut Butter with Grapes

Grab

Guacamole

1/2 avocado
1/2 medium tomato
1/8 onion
1/2 tablespoon chopped fresh
  cilantro
Juice from ½ of lime
Salt

Sides

1/2 apple
1 teaspoon of lemon juice mixed
  with 1/3 cup of water
1/2 cup grapes
1 oz tortilla chips
1 tablespoon peanut butter

Food Allergy Tips & Substitutions

For vegan and vegetarian diets and most allergies, adopt the substitution that fits your needs.

Swap peanut butter with soy nut butter or sunflower butter.

How to Make Guacamole

Dice avocado, tomato and onion and place in a small bowl. Add chopped cilantro, lime juice and a pinch of salt. Mix all ingredients together and pack in an air-tight container.

Packing Tip

Keep apples from turning brown by soaking them in lemon water for 20 seconds. Remember to pack an extra ice pack around the guacamole to keep it fresh and from turning brown before lunchtime.

Picky Eater Tip

If guacamole doesn't tickle your fancy, replace avocado with black beans. This will also add an extra burst of protein. Keep all other ingredients the same.

Larger Appetites

Drink plenty of water and eat slowly. This lunchbox is big enough to satisfy even the hungriest of appetites.

Total Lunchbox Nutrition Information

Calories 485, Total Fat 29, Sat Fat 4g, Trans Fat 0g, Cholesterol 0mg, Sodium 195mg, Carbohydrates 51g, Fiber 14g, Sugar 21g, Protein 9g, Vitamin A 12%, Calcium 8%, Vitamin C 37%, Iron 11%: Nutritional Grade B

Nutrition Tip

Although avocados are high in fat and have low amounts of protein, the fats they give us are healthy. Avocados also contain substantial amounts of potassium, fiber, folic acid and vitamins B and E.

3 Terrific Thursday

Chick'n Sandwich with Veggies, Graham Crackers and Oranges

Grab

Veggie Chick'n Burger

1 vegetable burger of your choice
1 100% whole-wheat hamburger
   bun
2 slices of tomatoes
8 leaves of lettuce
1 slice 2% American cheese
Ketchup
Mustard

Sides

1 cup 1% milk
1/3 cup mini graham crackers
1 orange
4 carrot sticks or mini carrots
4 celery sticks

Food Allergy Tips & Substitutions

For vegan and vegetarian diets and most allergies, adopt the substitution that fits your needs.

When purchasing your vegetable burger, read the label. Many are not vegan and can contain milk, eggs and soy. Swap regular milk and American cheese for your favorite non-dairy or vegan brands.

How to Make It

Fully cook chick'n burger in the microwave. Spread ketchup and mustard on both sides of bun. Top with cheese and chick'n burger and wrap the sandwich in foil or insulated container. Keep lettuce and tomato fresh by packing them on the side.

Packing Tip

Slice orange and pack other ingredients separately. Create your own semi-insulated container by wrapping the sandwich in foil, again in paper towel and again in foil. This will help keep it warm. Remember to pack it as far away from the cold ingredients in your lunchbox as possible.

Picky Eater Tip

Are you or your kids having a carrot and celery meltdown? That's OK; just swap the veggies with your favorites, like broccoli and tomatoes.

Feed the Sweet Tooth

Sprinkle a few raisins or maraschino cherries in with your orange if you're looking for a little something sweeter.

Total Lunchbox Nutrition Information

Calories 556, Total Fat 11.3, Sat Fat 3.6g, Trans Fat 0g, Cholesterol 0mg, Sodium 986mg, Carbohydrates 83g, Fiber 14g, Sugar 43g, Protein 32g, Vitamin A 155%, Calcium 68%, Vitamin C 175%, Iron 13%: Nutritional Grade A-

Nutrition Tip

Save a few extra calories by swapping out the 100% whole-wheat hamburger bun for a 100-calorie bagel or hamburger bun.

WEEK 3

3 Fun Friday

Apples and Peanut Butter with Pretzels, Cheese and Veggies with Dip

Grab

- 1 apple
- 1 tablespoon peanut butter
- 1 tablespoon low-fat ranch dressing
- 1/4 cup marble or cheddar cheese, diced
- 20 mini pretzel twists (one serving)
- 1/3 cup mini carrots or carrot sticks
- 1/3 cup snap peas
- 1 cup cold water
- 1/2 teaspoon lemon juice
- Sprinkle of cinnamon

Food Allergy Tips & Substitutions

For vegan and vegetarian diets and most allergies, adopt the substitution that fits your needs.

Swap the peanut butter with soy nut butter or sunflower butter. Replace cheddar cheese for your favorite dairy-free or vegan brand.

How to Make It
Wash, chop and core apple. To keep it from turning brown, combine lemon and water and soak apple for 20 seconds. Then remove from water, sprinkle cinnamon on top and pack in an airtight container.

Packing Tip
To save time, while your apple is soaking in lemon water, pack the remaining ingredients separately. Pack an extra ice pack to keep the ranch dressing at a safe temperature.

Picky Eater Tip
Snap peas can be hard to swallow for some kids. If this describes your little one, mix in their favorite vegetable, or replace the snap peas with cucumbers. You'll lose some of the fiber, but will keep the C and B vitamins.

Feed the Sweet Tooth
This lunchbox contains so many natural sugars from fruits and vegetables that you shouldn't need anything else. But, if you have a sweet tooth that can't be tamed, pack a piece of sugar-free gum.

Total Lunchbox Nutrition Information
Calories 486, Total Fat 17, Sat Fat 5g, Trans Fat 0g, Cholesterol 20mg, Sodium 821mg, Carbohydrates 68g, Fiber 10.1g, Sugar 27g, Protein 17g, Vitamin A 97%, Calcium 24%, Vitamin C 53%, Iron 14%: Nutritional Grade B+

Nutrition Tip

This lunchbox has 17 grams of protein! If you are normally a meat eater, go without it this time around. If that's difficult, add a serving of water-packed tuna on the side. But be calorie conscious and swap out the cheese or pretzels in its place.

Shopping List

Meatless Monday

Black Bean Burrito with Veggies, Oranges, Cottage Cheese

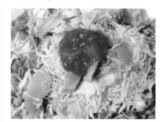

Tasty Tuesday

Taco Salad with Cheese, Avocado and Salsa

Wacky Wednesday

Spiral Festival Pasta with Strawberries and Whipped Cream

Terrific Thursday

Egg Salad Sandwich with Fruit and Pretzels

Fun Friday

Curry Chicken Sandwich with Watermelon and Carrots and Dip

Grocery

1 can black beans
Whole-wheat hamburger bun
100-calorie tortilla
Brown rice
Cumin
Curry powder
Salsa
Low-fat Italian dressing
Low-fat ranch dressing
Baked tortilla chips
Mini pretzel twists
Spiral veggie pasta
Frozen whole-kernel corn
Mayonnaise (or vegan alternative)

Produce

Avocado
Tomatoes
Cherry tomatoes
Leaf lettuce
Baby spinach
Leaf spinach
Broccoli florets
Romaine lettuce with vegetables (salad mix)
Snap peas
Carrots

Grated carrots
Orange
Tangerine
Grapes
Strawberries
Watermelon
Parsley (optional)
Raisins

Dairy

Low-fat Mexican-style cheese (or dairy-free alternative)
Low-fat cottage cheese (for vegan menu, use coleslaw or shredded red cabbage with vegan coleslaw dressing)
Low-fat cheddar cheese (or dairy-free alternative)
Light whipped topping (or dairy-free alternative)
Eggs *

Meat

Low-fat ground turkey (for vegan menu, use black beans or veggie taco crumbles)
1 chicken breast (or chicken seitan for vegan menu)

*Item is optional and can be replaced with Eggless Dill Salad, an optional meal substitution for vegan and vegetarian diets. The ingredients for this recipe are not on this list, but can be seen on page 72.

Prep Work

Week 4

4

20 minutes – 50 minutes

Review this week's menu.

Then use the following prep-work chart as a guide.
Modify it to fit your specific taste buds, fruit in season or on sale and recommended lunchbox allergy or food substitution as desired.

Task	Time	This Is For
Wash fruits and vegetables	2 minutes	Everyone
Slice carrots	3 minutes	Everyone
Hard-boil 2 eggs	12 minutes *	Everyone, except vegans
Dice watermelon	5 minutes *	Everyone
Bake chicken breast and dice into cubes	25 minutes *	Everyone, except vegans and vegetarians
Cook ground turkey	15 minutes	Everyone, except vegans and vegetarians
Rinse black beans	3 minutes	Everyone
Cook brown rice	20 minutes *	Everyone
Cook spiral pasta	15 minutes *	Everyone

*To save time, these items can be done in conjunction with other prep work such as chopping, dicing or pre-mixing ingredients.

4 Meatless Monday

Black Bean Burrito with Veggies, Oranges, Cottage Cheese and Broccoli

Grab

Black Bean Burrito

1/2 cup black beans, rinsed
1 large 100-calorie tortilla
1/4 chopped avocado
1/3 cup precooked brown rice
1/4 cup diced tomatoes
1/3 cup shredded baby spinach
2 tablespoons of low-fat Mexican-style cheese
Dash of cumin

Sides

1/3 cup low-fat cottage cheese
1 orange
1/3 cup broccoli florets and snap peas

Food Allergy Tips & Substitutions

For vegan and vegetarian diets and most allergies, adopt the substitution that fits your needs.

Eliminate or replace the Mexican style cheese with a dairy-free or vegan brand. Swap the cottage cheese for raw shredded red cabbage or coleslaw (using vegan salad dressing) for extra calcium.

How to Make It

Mix black beans, spinach, rice, tomato and dash of cumin together in a bowl and warm in the microwave for 1 minute. Next, using a damp paper towel as a cover, warm tortilla in the microwave for 15 seconds. The damp towel will help keep your tortilla from cracking when its folded. Place bean mixture on top of tortilla and top with cheese and avocado. Close burrito and wrap with foil, then wrap with paper towel and again with foil.

Packing Tip

Pack everything separately. Include extra ice packs to keep cottage cheese at a safe temperature.

Picky Eater Tip

Burritos can be hit or miss. But dip is almost a sure bet. To help a picky eater try something new, add a little salsa on the side for them to use for burrito dip. If you're having trouble eating cottage cheese, swap that out for low-fat ranch dip for the vegetables.

Larger Appetites

Portion sizes can be sneaky. This lunchbox is more than enough for most people. Drink more water if you're still hungry. For smaller appetites, cut the burrito in half and save 175 calories.

Total Lunchbox Nutrition Information

Calories 502, Total Fat 10, Sat Fat 1g, Trans Fat 0g, Cholesterol 3mg, Sodium 690mg, Carbohydrates 82g, Fiber 25g, Sugar 21g, Protein 26g, Vitamin A 36%, Calcium 39%, Vitamin C 197%, Iron 25%: Nutritional Grade A-

Nutrition Tip

Going meat-free once a week may reduce your risk of chronic preventable illnesses like cancer, cardiovascular disease, diabetes and obesity. Learn more about going meatless one day a week by visiting meatlessmonday.org.

4 Tasty Tuesday

Taco Salad with Cheese, Avocado and Salsa

Grab

Taco Salad

2 cups romaine lettuce with vegetables
1/3 cup low-fat ground turkey, cooked and seasoned
1/8 cup low-fat cheddar cheese
1/4 avocado
1/2 tomato
1 tablespoon salsa
2 tablespoons of your favorite low-fat Italian dressing

Side

1/3 cup crushed baked tortilla chips

Food Allergy Tips & Substitutions

For vegan and vegetarian diets and most allergies, adopt the substitution that fits your needs.

Eliminate or replace the cheese with a dairy-free or soy-free brand. Swap ground turkey for black beans or veggie taco crumbles.

How to Make It

Place lettuce/veggie mix in a bowl or container and add tomatoes. Give yourself a little extra room to add the rest of the salad ingredients during lunch. Warm cooked ground turkey in the microwave and pack separately in an insulated container.

Packing Tip

If you don't have an insulated container, make your own by wrapping an air-tight container in foil, then paper towel and again in foil. Pack the salsa, cheese, Italian dressing, chopped avocado and tortilla chips in separate containers.

Picky Eater Tip

Even kids who don't like salads will probably love this! Remember to show them how to assemble everything prior to packing their lunchbox. Once they start putting everything together, the anticipation of eating their creation will overcome their lack of enthusiasm to eat a salad.

Feed the Sweet Tooth

Although there is no fruit in this recipe, it's packed with 37 grams of protein and high amounts of calcium and vitamins A and C. A balanced meal like this usually kicks a sweet tooth's butt. But if you're still craving something sweet, add a mini box of raisins.

Total Lunchbox Nutrition Information

Calories 411, Total Fat 12, Sat Fat 2g, Trans Fat 0g, Cholesterol 400mg, Sodium 95mg, Carbohydrates 25g, Fiber 9g, Sugar 3g, Protein 37g, Vitamin A 151%, Calcium 19%, Vitamin C 45%, Iron 16%: Nutritional Grade A-
* Does not include salad dressing.

4 Wacky Wednesday

Spiral Festival Pasta with Strawberries and Whipped Cream

Grab

Spiral Festival Pasta

3/4 cup spiral veggie pasta, cooked
1/3 cup black beans, rinsed
1/8 cup grated carrots
1/8 cup frozen whole-kernel corn, thawed
4 cherry tomatoes
1/2 cup baby spinach, shredded
2 teaspoons olive oil
Salt
Pepper
Chopped parsley (optional)

Sides

4 strawberries
1/4 cup light whipped topping (frozen)

Food Allergy Tips & Substitutions

For vegan and vegetarian diets and most allergies, adopt the substitution that fits your needs.

Swap the whipped cream for your favorite non-dairy or vegan brand or replace it with non-dairy yogurt.

How to Make It

Combine cooked pasta, black beans, carrots, corn, cherry tomatoes, spinach, salt, pepper and olive oil and mix well. Top with chopped parsley and pack in a container.

Packing Tip

Pack strawberries and whipped cream separately in separate containers. Select whipped topping from the freezer section and include an extra ice pack to keep it fresh.

Feed the Sweet Tooth

The strawberries and whipped cream should feed the sweet tooth, but if you're looking for more, double its quantity. The extra 4 strawberries and whipped topping only adds 60 extra calories.

Larger Appetites

Add more beans, tomatoes, spinach or corn. Also, remember to drink plenty of water. This meal's portion size is excellent, so try not to overdo it. For younger kids, use half the pasta salad.

Total Lunchbox Nutrition Information

Calories 388, Total Fat 10, Sat Fat 1g, Trans Fat 0g, Cholesterol 0mg, Sodium 153mg, Carbohydrates 60g, Fiber 10g, Sugar 12g, Protein 12g, Vitamin A 141%, Calcium 8%, Vitamin C 86%, Iron 26%: Nutritional Grade A-

Nutrition Tip

High-protein pastas provide up to double the amount of protein than regular varieties. But, all pastas are not created equally, so read your nutrition labels. This lunchbox provides 12 grams of protein. Boost it to 16 grams by adding 1/4 cup of black beans.

4

Terrific Thursday

Egg Salad Sandwich with Fruit and Pretzels

Grab

Egg Salad Sandwich

2 slices of whole wheat bread
2 eggs, hardboiled
1 tablespoons mayonnaise
2 slices of tomatoes
8 leaves of lettuce
Salt
Pepper

Sides

1/3 cup mini pretzel twists
1/3 cup diced watermelon
1/2 tangerine
1/3 cup grapes

Food Allergy Tips & Substitutions

For vegan and vegetarian diets and most allergies, adopt the substitution that fits your needs.

Swap out the regular egg salad for our Eggless Dill Salad (pg 72).

How to Make It
Peel and dice the egg and place in a small bowl. Add mayonnaise, a pinch of salt and pepper. Combine and place mixture in a airtight container. Pack bread, lettuce and tomato separately.

Packing Tip
To prevent bread from getting soggy, let your kids assemble their sandwich. Include an ice pack to keep the egg salad cool. Combine fruit and place it in a leak-proof container. Pack pretzels separately.

Picky Eater Tip
Pick up a bread cutter tool at the dollar store to give your sandwich a neat design. Most kids agree that sandwiches shaped like dinosaurs, flowers and houses taste better!

Feed the Sweet Tooth
Although the fruit salad contains only 60 calories, it's packed with 12 grams of sugar. A natural and healthy boost to satisfy any sweet tooth!

Larger Appetites
Missing out on your favorite meat or just need a little something more? Spice it up by adding a piece of turkey bacon or veggie turkey bacon.

Total Lunchbox Nutrition Information
Calories 438, Total Fat 16, Sat Fat 4g, Trans Fat 0g, Cholesterol 0mg, Sodium 664mg, Carbohydrates 54g, Fiber 6g, Sugar 21g, Protein 21g, Vitamin A 25%, Calcium 14%, Vitamin C 32%, Iron 22%: Nutritional Grade A-

Nutrition Tip

Eggs are an excellent replacement to the traditional meat sandwich. The eggs in this lunchbox provide 11 grams of protein. Select high-protein bread and you'll be getting 21 grams of protein in this meal.

4 Fun Friday

Curry Chicken Sandwich with Watermelon and Carrots and Dip

Grab

Curry Chicken Sandwich

1 100% whole-wheat hamburger bun
1/3 cup diced chicken
1 tablespoon mayonnaise
1/2 teaspoon curry powder
1 tablespoon raisins

Sides

1 cup chopped watermelon
1 tablespoon low-fat ranch dressing
1/3 cup carrots, sliced

Food Allergy Tips & Substitutions

For vegan and vegetarian diets and most allergies, adopt the substitution that fits your needs.

Use vegan mayonnaise. Swap ranch dressing for hummus or sunflower seeds. Replace diced chicken with seasoned tempeh.

How to Make It

Combine diced chicken, mayonnaise, curry powder and raisins in a bowl and mix well. Place mixture on top of one side of hamburger bun, and add lettuce and tomato on the other side. Then close sandwich and place in a container.

Packing Tip

Remember to add an ice pack to keep the dressing fresh and at a safe temperature.

Picky Eater Tip

Unlike traditional bread, and its pesky crust, most kids love hamburger buns. Keep this lunchbox hassle-free by using a hamburger bun.

Feed the Sweet Tooth

Your sweet tooth should be on vacation during this lunchbox meal. But, if it's calling your name, drink a little extra water. It mixes well with the watermelon's natural juices to fill cravings with no added calories.

Larger Appetites

Increase the portion size healthfully by doubling up on carrots or adding a couple tablespoons of sunflower seeds.

Total Lunchbox Nutrition Information

Calories 444, Total Fat 13g, Sat Fat 2g, Trans Fat 0g, Cholesterol 40mg, Sodium 562mg, Carbohydrates 62g, Fiber 8g, Sugar 20g, Protein 24g, Vitamin A 141%, Calcium 14%, Vitamin C 25%, Iron 18%: Nutritional Grade A-

Nutrition Tip

Raisins are an excellent energy source and digestion aid. If your taste buds allow, leave them in this lunchbox. If not, pack another fiber-rich food on the side such as figs or berries.

Shopping List

week 5

5

Meatless Monday

Red Bean Dip with Flat Pretzels, Pineapple and Veggies

Tasty Tuesday

Salmon Salad with Cheese, Veggies, Watermelon and Grapes

Wacky Wednesday

Dancing Pasta with Ants on a Log and a Tangerine

Terrific Thursday

Chicken Sub with Whole Grain Chips, Blueberries and a Tangerine

Fun Friday

Cheese and Crackers with Chicken, Broccoli and Fruit

Grocery

Canned red kidney beans (or garbanzo beans)
Mayonnaise (or vegan alternative)
Mustard
Rice wine vinegar
Pretzel Chips (or regular pretzels)
Whole-wheat hot dog bun
Whole-wheat crackers
Italian dressing
Frozen whole-kernel corn
Protein-enriched spiral pasta
Peanut butter (substitute low-fat cream cheese, soy butter or sunflower butter for nut allergy issues)
Tortilla chips

Produce

Celery
Yellow onion
Tomato
Cherry tomatoes
Cucumber
Celery

Baby spinach
Leaf spinach
Parsley
Carrots
Broccoli florets
Diced pineapple
Watermelon
2 tangerines
Blueberries
Grapes
Apple
Raisins

Dairy

2 fresh mozzarella cheese balls or one string cheese stick (or non-dairy alternative)
1% low-fat mozzarella cheese
Low-fat marbled cheese cubes

Meat

5-ounce package pink salmon
Chicken breast strips (substitute tempeh or veggie burger)
1 chicken breast (substitute tempeh or veggie bacon

Prep Work

week 5

5

10 minutes – 1 hour

Review this week's menu.

Then use the following prep-work chart as a guide.
Modify it to fit your specific taste buds, fruit in season (or on sale)
and recommended lunchbox allergy or food substitution as
desired.

Task	Time	This Is For
Wash fruits and vegetables	2 minutes	Everyone
Dice carrots, celery, onions and broccoli	5 minutes	Everyone
Dice pineapple and watermelon	7 minutes	Everyone
Bake chicken breast and dice into cubes	25 minutes *	Everyone, except vegans and vegetarians
Rinse black beans	3 minutes	Everyone
Cook spiral pasta	15 minutes *	Everyone

*To save time, these items can be done in conjunction with other
prep work such as chopping, dicing, or pre-mixing ingredients.

This Food Loves You

5 Meatless Monday

Red Bean Dip with Flat Pretzels, Pineapple and Veggies

Grab

Red Bean Dip

1/2 cup drained and rinsed red kidney beans
1 tablespoon finely chopped celery
1 tablespoon finely chopped onions
1/2 tablespoon chopped fresh parsley
1 tablespoon mayonnaise
1/4 teaspoon rice wine vinegar
Salt and pepper to taste

Sides

1/3 cup diced pineapple
1/2 cup pretzel chips
1/2 cup broccoli florets and chopped carrots

Food Allergy Tips & Substitutions

For vegan and vegetarian diets and most allergies, adopt the substitution that fits your needs.

Swap regular mayonnaise for vegan mayonnaise.

How to Make It
Combine mayonnaise with rice wine vinegar in a small bowl and mix well. Add beans, chopped celery, onion, parsley and salt and pepper to taste. Mix well and place in an airtight container.

Packing Tip
To keep the Red Bean Dip at a safe temperature, include an ice pack when packing this lunchbox.

Picky Eater Tip
If your kid isn't a red bean lover, swap them for garbanzo beans. Keep other ingredients the same.

Feed the Sweet Tooth
Add 1/2 cup of pineapple. Your sweet tooth will be satisfied for only 30 extra calories.

Larger Appetites
Include a rice cake in this lunchbox if you need a little something more. Depending upon the variety, you'll only be adding 35-50 extra calories.

Total Lunchbox Nutrition Information
Calories 361, Total Fat 5, Sat Fat .8g, Trans Fat 0g, Cholesterol 4mg, Sodium 700mg, Carbohydrates 66g, Fiber 12.7g, Sugar 11.9g, Protein 14.3g, Vitamin A 5%, Calcium 4%, Vitamin C 49%, Iron 16%:
Nutritional Grade B+

Nutrition Tip

Keep kidney beans in this lunchbox if you can. They provide an excellent source of iron, complex carbohydrates and fiber, which are all terrific nutritional components to this meal.

5 Tasty Tuesday

Salmon Salad with Cheese, Veggies, Watermelon and Grapes

Grab

Salmon Salad

1 5-ounce package of pink salmon
   (or canned for multiple lunches)
1/2 tomato, chopped
1/4 cup cucumber, chopped
1/8 cup frozen corn, thawed
Salt and pepper, to taste
Parsley (optional)

Spinach and Cheese Salad

1 cup fresh baby spinach
2 fresh mozzarella cheese balls
   (or one stick of string cheese,
   chopped in quarters)
1 tablespoon chopped carrots

Food Allergy Tips & Substitutions

For vegan and vegetarian diets and most allergies, adopt the substitution that fits your needs.

Replace mozzarella cheese balls for sesame seeds or non-dairy cheese. Swap salmon with black beans or tofu. If using tofu, I highly recommend adding garlic, a tablespoon of chopped onions and a fresh herb such as dill, cilantro or parsley.

How to Make Salmon Salad

Drain salmon and place it in a small bowl. Add chopped tomato, cucumber and corn. Mix and top with parsley (optional). Pack in an airtight leak-proof container.

How to Make Spinach and Cheese Salad

Place baby spinach in a bowl and layer with carrots and mozzarella cheese balls.

Packing Tip

To keep watermelon and salad from leaking use airtight containers. Pack salad dressing separately and include at least two ice packs to keep everything fresh and safe to eat.

Picky Eater Tip

If you're having trouble getting your little ones to eat spinach salad, combine Salmon Salad with the Spinach and Cheese salad to make one entrée. The only modification needed is to cut the baby spinach and mozzarella cheese balls into small pieces.

Feed the Sweet Tooth

By increasing watermelon to 1/2 cup, you'll add only 25 extra calories.

Total Lunchbox Nutrition Information

Calories 436, Total Fat 21.1g, Sat Fat 9.1g, Trans Fat 0g, Cholesterol 80mg, Sodium 467mg, Carbohydrates 32g, Fiber 2.6g, Sugar 11.6g, Protein 35.2g, Vitamin A 97%, Calcium 27%, Vitamin C 41%, Iron 17%: Nutritional Grade C+

Nutrition Tip

Bump this meal up a notch to a nutritional grade B by substituting a string cheese stick for the whole milk mozzarella cheese balls. You'll save almost 120 calories and 13 grams of fat.

5 Wacky Wednesday

Dancing Pasta with Ants on a Log and a Tangerine

Grab

Dancing Pasta

1/2 cup protein enriched spiral pasta
6 cherry tomatoes, halved
1/3 cup chopped carrots
1/3 cup chopped broccoli
Salt and pepper to taste
1/4 cup low-fat 1% mozzarella cheese

Ants on a Log

2 4-inch stalks of celery
1 tablespoon peanut butter
1 tablespoon raisins

Food Allergy Tips & Substitutions

For vegan and vegetarian diets and most allergies, adopt the substitution that fits your needs.

Swap the peanut butter for sunflower butter, soy nut butter or low-fat cream cheese.

How to Make Dancing Pasta
Combine spiral pasta with tomatoes, carrots, cheese and broccoli in a small bowl. Add salt and pepper.

How to Make Ants on a Log
Put 1/2 tablespoon of peanut butter on each celery stalk and top with raisins.

Packing Tip
If your little one is assembling this lunch herself, pack the celery, peanut butter and raisins separately. Remember to include a plastic knife in the lunchbox.

Picky Eater Tip
Celery can be hit or miss with many people. If it's a miss in your house, swap it out for half an apple. This will add 40-50 extra calories to your lunchbox. If this concerns you, eliminate the raisins and save 30 calories, almost breaking even.

Feed the Sweet Tooth
This lunchbox packs 21 grams of healthy natural sugar; I doubt you'll need more sweetness.

Larger Appetites
Add two celery sticks. Without increasing the amount of peanut butter, you'll feel like you're eating more food, but only increasing your calorie intake by 5.

Total Lunchbox Nutrition Information
Calories 413, Total Fat 15.2, Sat Fat 5.3g, Trans Fat 0g, Cholesterol 15mg, Sodium 310mg, Carbohydrates 53g, Fiber 9g, Sugar 21g, Protein 20g, Vitamin A 146%, Calcium 31%, Vitamin C 147%, Iron 16%: Nutritional Grade A-

Nutrition Tip

Dairy products interfere with the absorption of iron in the body. If you want to increase your iron intake but still need calcium, swap out the cheese and double the amount of fresh broccoli—it's an excellent source of calcium.

WEEK 5

5 Terrific Thursday

Chicken Sub with Whole-Grain Chips, Blueberries and a Tangerine

Grab

Chicken Sub

1 100% whole-wheat hot dog bun
4 pieces of chicken breast strips
3 slices of tomatoes
8 spinach leaves
1 tablespoon mayonnaise
1 teaspoon mustard
1 tablespoon low-fat shredded
   mozzarella cheese

Sides

1 tangerine
1/4 cup blueberries
1 cup tortilla chips (one serving)
4 large slices of cucumbers

Food Allergy Tips & Substitutions

For vegan and vegetarian diets and most allergies, adopt the substitution that fits your needs.

Eliminate or replace shredded mozzarella cheese for non-dairy or vegan cheese. Swap regular mayonnaise for vegan mayonnaise. Substitute chicken breast strips for tempeh or sliced veggie chicken burger.

How to Make It

Spread mayonnaise and mustard on bun. Add spinach, tomato and cheese. Top with chicken. Wrap in foil or pack in an airtight container.

Packing Tip

Stimulate your little ones sight and smell by combining the tangerine with blueberries. Pack everything else separately and remember to include two ice packs to keep your sandwich cool and safe to eat.

Picky Eater Tip

Kids can often be very particular with what type of raw veggies they'll eat. If this describes your little one, swap the cucumber for his or her favorite vegetable.

Feed the Sweet Tooth

Fruit out of season can be tart or less flavorful. Remedy this problem swap this recipe's fruits for ones in season. Or mix in 2 tablespoons of whipped cream.

Larger Appetites

This meal is pretty hearty. If you're still hungry, increase your water intake.

Total Lunchbox Nutrition Information

Calories 525, Total Fat 16.9, Sat Fat 1.8g, Trans Fat 0g, Cholesterol 54mg, Sodium 678mg, Carbohydrates 64g, Fiber 610.4g, Sugar 16g, Protein 31.8g, Vitamin A 159%, Calcium 30%, Vitamin C 139%, Iron 36%: Nutritional Grade A

Nutrition Tip

Save up to 100 calories and
turn this sub into a wrap. Simply
swap out the hot dog bun for a
100-calorie whole-wheat tortilla.

5 Fun Friday

Cheese and Crackers with Chicken, Broccoli and Fruit

Grab

- 10 whole-wheat crackers
- 1/3 cup low-fat marble cubed cheese
- 3/4 cup watermelon
- 1/4 cup blueberries
- 1 apple
- 1 tablespoon peanut butter
- 1/3 cup chopped broccoli
- 1/3 cup chopped chicken breast
- 1 cup cold water
- 1 teaspoon lemon or lime juice
- Dash of cinnamon (optional)

Food Allergy Tips & Substitutions

For vegan and vegetarian diets and most allergies, adopt the substitution that fits your needs.

Swap cubed cheese for sesame seeds. Replace peanut butter for soy nut butter or sunflower butter. Substitute chicken breast for veggie bacon or tempeh.

How to Make It

Chop apple and soak it in lemon water for 20-30 seconds, remove from water and sprinkle with a dash of cinnamon. While it's soaking, combine watermelon and blueberries and then chicken and broccoli. Pack everything separately.

Packing Tip

Cinnamon adds a little jazz to your apple, but if your little one doesn't like its flavor, don't fret. Simply replace it with ginger, nutmeg or pumpkin pie spice.

Picky Eater Tip

There are a lot of main characters in this lunchbox. Keep taste buds interested and create a tantalizing food display by packing everything separately.

Feed the Sweet Tooth

If your sweet tooth is still hungry after this lunchbox, it might be time to do a sugar detox! This lunchbox is packed full of 29 grams of healthy natural sugars.

Larger Appetites

This lunchbox is deceivingly filling. If you typically eat more food, try something new. Swap out your desire to add more with a concentrated effort to eat slowly and enjoy this Fun Friday creation, one bite at a time.

Total Lunchbox Nutrition Information

Calories 563, Total Fat 21.4, Sat Fat 6.3g, Trans Fat 0g, Cholesterol 63mg, Sodium 95mg, Carbohydrates 66g, Fiber 10g, Sugar 35g, Protein 31g, Vitamin A 25%, Calcium 52%, Vitamin C 80%, Iron 19%: Nutritional Grade B+

Nutrition Tip

If your picky eater has a green color aversion, then swap the broccoli with red bell pepper (high in vitamin C, but less nutrients like vitamins A and K, potassium and iron). Try introducing green veggies into his or her diet at another opportunity.

Substitution Recipes

Eggless Dill Salad

Grab

1 block of extra firm tofu
1/3 cup Vegeniase
1/4 cup shredded carrots
1/4 cup chopped celery
1/3 cup chopped onions
2 tablespoons chopped dill
Salt and pepper to taste

This was one of the first vegan dishes I created. It's extremely versatile and can be eaten as a dip, in a sandwich or rolled into a tortilla. My kids love it eaten with spinach, sitting on top of crackers.

How to Make It

1. Drain water out of the tofu package. Then cut it in half lengthwise and wrap each piece in a clean towel for 30 minutes to soak out additional water.
2. Mash drained tofu in a bowl with the back of your fork. Continue to mash until all the large pieces are gone.
3. Add the remaining ingredients to the tofu bowl and mix well.
4. Tastes best when chilled in the refrigerator for at least one hour, but can be eaten immediately and stored up to four days.

Time-saving Tip

Prepare tofu and chop veggies with the rest of your prep-work to keep it a 5-minute lunchbox meal.

Substitution Recipes

Do-It-Yourself Granola a.k.a. Giraffe Granola

Grab

- 2 cups oatmeal
- 1/2 cup carrot pulp leftover from juicing (or ¼ cup grated carrots, air-dried for 2 hours)
- 1/2 cup raisins
- 1/2 cup shaved coconut, no sugar added (optional)
- 2 tablespoons brown sugar
- 1 teaspoon cinnamon
- 1 teaspoon vanilla
- 2 tablespoons flaxseed
- 2 tablespoons maple syrup
- 2 tablespoons canola oil
- Pinch of salt

I created this recipe for Healthy Little Cooks' Weekend Food Challenge, when carrot was the featured ingredient. Since then, it's been one of our most famous recipes. An excellent option for anyone that needs to control the amount of sugar in their food and for kids with nut or tree nut allergies. My son who eats a gluten-free and nut-free diet swears by this recipe. My husband with no allergies loves it also!

How to Make It

1. Preheat oven to 325.
2. Mix oatmeal, raisins, carrot pulp, flaxseed, brown sugar, shaved coconut, cinnamon and salt in a bowl. Mix maple syrup, canola oil and vanilla extract in a separate bowl and pour over oatmeal mixture. Stir well so all of the oatmeal is coated with your maple syrup mix.
5. Spread the oats on a baking sheet and bake for 15 minutes.
6. Then stir and bake for another 12-18 minutes. (Cooking for a total of 27-33 minutes).
7. Remove from baking sheet and pour into an airtight storage container.
Makes 12 servings.

Time-saving Tip

Prepare while doing your weekly prep-work to keep it a 5-minute lunchbox meal.

Get More.

Download a
FREE Bonus week of recipes at:

www.HealthyLittleCooks.com

Cut-out Weekly Shopping Lists

The following pages were designed to be cut out and taken with you to the grocery store to make shopping easier with a pre-made check list. You can review each week's menu, then modify this shopping list according to your dietary needs, specific taste buds, and fruit in season or on sale.

Review the week's menu. Then modify this shopping list according to your dietary needs, specific taste buds, fruit in season or on sale.

Grocery

___Hummus
___100-calorie whole-wheat tortillas
___Mayonnaise (regular or vegan)
___Mustard
___Pretzel sticks
___Applesauce (unsweetened)
___Granola
___Sunflower butter (optional)
___1 tablespoon sesame seeds
___2 baked mini breadsticks
___Raisins
___Marinara sauce
___100-calorie whole-wheat bagel
___Whole-wheat pita pocket
___Plantain chips (optional)
___Low-fat granola bar
___Kabob sticks

Produce

___1 avocado
___1 cup spinach
___Raw almonds (optional)
___Precut romaine lettuce with mixed vegetables
___Cherry tomatoes
___1 cucumber
___Watermelon
___Cantaloupe
___Honeydew melon
___Grapes
___Pineapple
___Strawberries
___1 apple
___1 stalk celery
___Carrots
___Dried mango slices

Dairy

___Eggs
___1/4 cup 2% shredded mozzarella cheese
___Fat-free Greek vanilla yogurt

Meat

___1 chicken breast or
___6 ounces frozen precooked breast strips (or veggie chicken)

Substitution Items

Week 2

2 Shopping List

Review the week's menu. Then modify this shopping list according to your dietary needs, specific taste buds, fruit in season or on sale.

Grocery

___100-calorie whole-wheat bagels
___Whole-wheat bread
___Whole-wheat hot dog buns
___Whole-wheat raisin English muffin
___Jelly of your choice
___Brown rice
___Black beans
___Mustard
___Mayonnaise
___Marinara sauce
___Mini pretzel twists
___Low-fat popcorn
___Peanut butter
___Low-fat ranch dressing

Produce

___Cucumber
___Tomatoes
___Cherry tomatoes
___Shredded carrots
___Red onion
___Romaine lettuce
___Apple
___Grapes
___Strawberries
___Blueberries
___Leaf spinach
___Tangerines
___Pineapple
___Almonds (optional)
___Sunflower seeds (optional)
___Watermelon
___Broccoli
___Shaved almonds

Dairy

___Low-fat feta cheese
___Yogurt
___String cheese (optional)
___Low-fat mozzarella cheese
___Low-fat cream cheese

Meat

___Veggie bacon
___Pre-cooked turkey meatballs

Substitution Items

Shipping List
Week 3

Review the week's menu. Then modify this shopping list according to your dietary needs, specific taste buds, fruit in season or on sale.

Grocery

___Whole-wheat bread
___Whole-wheat bagel
___Whole-wheat hamburger bun
___Rice crispy treat
___Mini graham crackers
___Cashews
___Barbecue sauce
___Low-fat Italian dressing
___Low-fat ranch dressing
___Pretzel sticks
___Mini pretzel twists
___Tortilla chips
___Peanut butter
___Lemon juice
___Ketchup
___Mustard
___Cinnamon

Produce

___Cucumber
___Avocado
___Tomato
___Lettuce
___Yellow onion
___Cherry tomatoes
___Shredded red cabbage
___Baby spinach
___Carrot sticks or Mini Carrots
___Celery sticks
___Snap peas
___Dried dill or chives
___Cilantro
___Lime
___Grapes
___Apple
___Orange
___Strawberries
___Blueberries

Dairy

___Whipped cream cheese
___Low-fat shredded mozzarella cheese
___2% milk American cheese slices
___Low-fat marble cheese or Cheddar cheese
___1% milk

Meat

___1 chicken breast
___Veggie burger

Substitution Items

Week 4

4 Shopping List

Review the week's menu. Then modify this shopping list according to your dietary needs, specific taste buds, fruit in season or on sale.

Grocery

___1 can black beans
___Whole-wheat hamburger bun
___100-calorie tortilla
___Brown rice
___Cumin
___Curry powder
___Salsa
___Low-fat Italian dressing
___Low-fat ranch dressing
___Baked tortilla chips
___Mini pretzel twists
___Spiral veggie pasta
___Frozen whole-kernel corn
___Mayonnaise

Produce

___Avocado
___Tomatoes
___Cherry tomatoes
___Leaf lettuce
___Baby spinach
___Leaf spinach
___Broccoli florets
___Romaine lettuce with vegetables (salad mix)
___Snap peas
___Carrots
___Grated carrots
___Orange
___Tangerine
___Grapes
___Strawberries
___Watermelon
___Parsley (optional)
___Raisins

Dairy

___Low-fat Mexican-style cheese
___Low-fat cottage cheese
___Low-fat cheddar cheese
___Light whipped topping

Meat

___Low-fat ground turkey
___1 chicken breast

Substitution Items

Week 5

5 Shopping List

Review the week's menu. Then modify this shopping list according to your dietary needs, specific taste buds, fruit in season or on sale.

Grocery

___Canned red kidney beans (or garbanzo beans)
___Mayonnaise
___Rice wine vinegar
___Pretzel Chips (or regular pretzels)
___Whole-wheat hot dog bun
___Whole-wheat crackers
___Italian dressing
___Frozen whole-kernel corn
___Protein-enriched spiral pasta
___Peanut butter
___Tortilla chips

Produce

___Celery
___Yellow onion
___Tomato
___Cherry tomatoes
___Cucumber
___Celery
___Baby spinach
___Leaf spinach
___Parsley
___Carrots
___Broccoli florets
___Diced pineapple
___Watermelon
___2 tangerines
___Blueberries
___Grapes
___Apple
___Raisins

Dairy

___2 fresh mozzarella balls
___1% low-fat mozzarella cheese
___Low-fat marbled cheese cubes

Meat

___5-ounce package pink salmon
___Chicken breast strips
___1 chicken breast

Substitution Items

You're Awesome! Thank you for taking the journey with me to become a healthier food advocate for yourself and your children.

Made in the USA
Lexington, KY
01 September 2015